Grounded Presents

Defining Moments

Stories of Strength, Courage, & Hope

Compiled by Dr. Aleta V. Ashford

INCESSANT
Incessant Publishing, LLC.

DEDICATION

This book is written in tribute to Josie Mae Roddy, a remarkable woman who envisioned a bright future for her family that extended far beyond her time.

Table Of Contents

1. THE SOUND OF MY SALVATION   1

2. PURPOSED IN VICTORY   13

3. GOD HAS THE FINAL SAY   29

4. YOUR STORY IS GOD'S GLORY   38

5. BEAUTIFULLY BROKEN WARRIOR   49

6. BEYOND THE SURFACE   58

7. A SONG IN MY HEART   67

8. GREAT IS GOD'S FAITHFULNESS   74

9. NO OBSTACLE TOO BIG   86

10. BIRTHING A CAN'T   99

11. THROUGH MY EYES   109

FOREWORD

My name is Laverne C. Allen, and I have the distinct pleasure and honor of presenting the esteemed Dr. Aleta, V. Ashford, who is a successful business owner, author, writer, educator, podcaster, and motivational speaker. Dr. Ashford is a wife and mother who has been happily married for over ten years, and our friendship has remained constant throughout this time.

Though one could easily Google all of Dr. Ashford's achievements, this would not explain how creative, loving, intelligent, and modest she is, as well as how fortunate I am to know her. Dr. Ashford is truly one of the kindest people I have ever known. As her friend and mentor, I have watched Dr. Ashford grow and develop as a person and my life has been brightened by her infectious zest for life and unwavering belief that anything is possible.

The words and insight that Dr. Ashford has shared with me over the years have positively impacted my life. Her message to "surround yourself with joyful friends" is a philosophy that I have personally adopted. An overcomer, Dr. Ashford has managed to keep her head held high above the clamor, and the noise of her critics. Gifted in her own right, her personality exudes the essence of other greats such as the extremely talented Oprah Winfrey and the highly decorated Condoleezza Rice, as her accomplishments and professional achievements would be just as outstanding if listed here.

Dr. Ashford is a consummate professional and an even better human being, not to mention she is funny, witty, well-traveled, and a didactical learner self-taught in the areas of writing, multi-media, and podcasting all of which are a few of her exceptional abilities.

Most profound is Dr. Ashford's faith, which in some instances is comparable to the size of a mustard seed and has been an inspiration to me personally. In addition to being a Christian, Dr. Ashford is also the Founder of Grounded Jeremiah 29:11, a faith-based platform she created to glorify God and unite women around the world. Because of her efforts and willingness to use her gifts for the betterment of others, countless businesses, ministries, careers, and dreams have been realized. The book you are about to read is no exception. This book is a creative aspiration featuring the women of Grounded Jeremiah 29:11, some of whom are first-time authors. Just another example of Dr. Ashford's vision and continued desire to make the world a better place by helping others.

Laverne C. Allen

Laverne C. Allen is a remarkable woman who has achieved success both professionally and in her personal life. In addition to a thriving corporate career, Laverne is a devoted mother and grandmother, currently residing in Orlando, Florida, where she enjoys spending quality time with her loved ones.

Laverne is first and foremost a Christian and dedicated member of her church where she finds great fulfillment in serving others and spreading positivity throughout her community. Laverne is also an active volunteer in her local area, where she works to make a difference in the lives of those around her. Her kind and selfless nature make her a beloved member of her community and a true inspiration to others.□

PREFACE

For a long time, I regretted the number of years I wasted before finally stepping out on faith to publish my first book. Now looking back, I can attest that the time I spent waiting was not wasted at all. My waiting was a season of preparation in which God had allowed me time to grow my gifts and develop the ability to not only write books but also to self-publish and be placed in a position to help other women.

Since deciding to step out on faith, the desire I have to help other women has expanded to include Grounded Jeremiah 29:11, a faith-based women's group that was formed during the height of the pandemic. Since launching in September of 2021, Grounded has since grown from a platform highlighting the works of women business owners, authors, artists, and ministry leaders; to a network of ministries supporting the personal and professional growth of women, all while uplifting the Gospel of Jesus Christ.

Most recently, Grounded Jeremiah 29:11 has expanded to include a book club highlighting women authors as well as introducing the "Grounded Presents" podcast now streaming on all major platforms. This book, comprised of inspirational stories featuring the women of Grounded, is a symbol of God's glory as well as the first of many books of its kind to follow.

Dr. Aleta V. Ashford, Founder of Grounded Jeremiah 29:11

INTRODUCTION

In the heart of every struggle lies the potential for an extraordinary story of triumph. This book is a testament to the power of resilience, faith, and the unyielding human spirit. It is a collection of stories that celebrate the victories of women who have faced unimaginable challenges and emerged stronger, wiser, and more determined. One such story is my own...

At the age of eighteen, I ran away from home and fell into a lifestyle of addiction, unhealthy relationships, and constant searching for love in the wrong places. Methamphetamine eventually took over my life, leading to homelessness and erratic behavior.

To simply say that meth had taken control of my life would be an understatement. Meth didn't just take control of my life; it consumed it entirely. It left me homeless, addicted, and wandering the streets. Every breath I took was in pursuit of my next high. I worshiped this destructive force as if it were a god, an idol above all others.

The turning point came when I ended up in jail and faced a judge who gave me the choice to either get my life together or go to prison. Choosing to fight for my life, I embarked on a difficult journey of recovery with God's help. While the full details of my journey are too extensive to cover here, know this: the battle was won. GOD fought for me and helped me overcome my addiction.

Once I decided to climb out of the pit of destruction that my life had become, God stepped in and cleaned up the mess I had made. It's incredible to think about, especially since I barely knew Him at the time.□

This book is not just about my journey. It is about the journeys of many women who have faced their own battles and emerged victorious. Their stories are a testament to the strength and courage it takes to overcome adversity. They remind us that no matter how dark the path may seem, there is always hope, and with faith and determination, we can triumph over any obstacle.

As you read these stories, may you find inspiration and strength. May you see the power of resilience and the beauty of transformation. And may you be reminded that your story, too, has the power to inspire and change the world.

Sue Michael Carter

Sue Michael Carter, affectionally known as "Mama Sue", is 77 years old and a resident of Orlando, Florida. In addition to being a woman of faith, Mama Sue is a mother, grandmother, and great-grandmother as well as an overcomer who has committed a considerable portion of her life toward encouraging young women to achieve their goals.

A former caterer and owner of a daycare; Sue Michael Carter is the owner and operator of All Dolled Up Accessory LLC. and a key contributor to Grounded Jeremiah 29:11 where she takes her role as a ministry leader very seriously. Through her strength and dedication, Mama Sue has served in various areas of her community and continues to thrive and reach new heights.

Recently, Mama Sue began the process of going back to school and is a gleaming example that it is never too late to pursue the plans and purposes that God has for your life.

THE SOUND OF MY SALVATION

By Dr. Aleta V. Ashford

Some of the most inspirational stories I've ever heard have often been stories that are themed with some element of pain, struggle, or adversity. My story is no different. As a young woman, I often struggled to find my place in the world. In fact, if I were to describe my childhood, the two words that come to mind are dark and lonely. I wasn't born into a perfect family, and truth be told for most of my life I never really felt like I belonged anywhere.

As a survivor of sexual abuse, neglect, and trauma that I experienced throughout various phases of my life; I had long learned to hide the dark, shameful, prisms of the past. Invisible scars of my youth that I had buried, carried, and did my best to conceal and heal from. The only thing in my life that has ever been certain was an overwhelming feeling

I had that I was meant to be somewhere else. Meant to be someone else.

It started at an early age when my father often told me that I would one day go to college and have a successful corporate career. At the time, I didn't understand much of what was being said. However, when my father spoke about the future it was always with strong conviction, so much so that I believed him. As imperfect as he was, my father was always teaching me something. He had high hopes for my future and with his words had fueled ambition in me long before I was old enough to understand the impact that they would have on my life.

As a young girl, my father would often take me to a small town located in Bainbridge, Georgia to visit his mother, Josie, whom everyone affectionally called Grandma Bill. Like my father, my grandmother used our time together to implant knowledge that often made no sense to me as a child. It was almost as if she knew that I would one day need her wisdom. What I recall most about my grandmother was her strength. Grandma Bill was strong, independent, and knew how to survive. Though Grandma did not have much, the one thing she did have was her faith which she sprinkled into our interactions every time I came to visit.

My earliest memories of attending church were around 5 years old. Every Sunday, Grandma Bill would gather all the grandchildren, dress us up, and take us down to an old wooden building. Before we left the house, Grandma Bill would always place a few pennies in each of our hands for the offering; and at the beginning of every service, she would always pull out a single stick of gum that she divided between five grandkids. To most, a small piece of gum doesn't sound like much, but to us grandkids it was golden.

Even now I reflect fondly upon these memories and have often wondered if my grandmother knew that I would one day find my way to Christ. What she will never know, however, is the countless times that I have reverted to these memories for strength, courage, and hope during some of the darkest moments in my life.

By my early twenties, my father and Grandma Bill had both passed on and with them any dreams I had of going to college much less doing anything of significance with my life. As a young woman, I often felt lost and found my self-esteem in clubs and the empty arms of strangers. For the most part, I didn't feel special or important and had long forgotten the words of my father and grandmother. By my mid-twenties, I had already had one failed marriage and was on the brink of suicide when I had an encounter with Jesus.

It was one of the lowest points in my life. That is, the day I planned to end it all. I was 24 years old and in the process of relocating and starting my life over. I was scheduled to board a plane the following morning when I suddenly began to experience an overwhelming sense of fear and anxiety about the future. Embarking on this new chapter of my life would be the first time that I had ever done anything on my own as an adult and I was terrified.

In some ways I felt like a child in a grown woman's body, journeying to a place I had never been before with no one waiting for me on the other side. The more I pondered over factors such as having no job, very little money, and no friends or family where I was going; The more convinced I became that I would not be able to survive. At that moment I thought that my life would be a lot easier if I just ended it.

It wasn't long before I had gathered every pill I had in the apartment and lined them up across the floor next to a bottle of vodka. This was it. As I sat there staring at the colorful array of pills and capsules before me, random thoughts of my fears, failures, and the most shameful parts of my past flashed through my mind like a picture show with a sad ending.

I must have laid there for hours sobbing before crying out to the God that I had only experienced the few times my grandmother took me to church as a child. I had just reached over to pick up a handful of pills when unexpectedly, the phone rang.

In the dead silence of that moment, the sound of the phone ringing came through like a resounding trumpet with an intensity that drowned out any notions I had that I could disappear, and no one would notice that I was gone. Instead, the phone ringing was confirmation that someone somewhere was thinking of me. Most importantly, it was evident that God had heard my prayers and answered with the most beautiful sound I had ever heard... The sound of my salvation.

On the other end of the call was a former friend that I had not connected with in a while. She had recently given her life to Christ and was calling to invite me to a church revival. At the time I didn't know what a revival was, but on the same day that I had planned to end my life, I attended a church service and gave my life to Christ that very night.

The following morning, I woke with a new sense of hope that I had never experienced before. As I entered this new phase of my life, negative thoughts that had once overwhelmed me slowly faded to the positive affirmations of my father, grandmother, and the Pastor who had assured me the night before that "There is no place you can go where God won't be." Words that I never forgot and have kept with me since that fateful night.

Becoming a Christian completely changed my life. Over time I gained confidence, and self-esteem, and transformed into a woman with values who respected herself and her body. For the first time in my life, I had standards and was proud of the person I was becoming. By the grace of God, I even made it to college and started my corporate career just as my father had envisioned I would. I went on to become a mother to a beautiful baby boy and later married a wonderful man whom God sent to help me raise him.

As I reflect on my life then and now, I am often reminded of a popular game show where contestants are given the option of taking a cash prize or choosing what's behind a mysterious curtain. Most contestants are quick to assume that the first option (usually cash) is their best option only to discover that there are other (more appealing) alternatives waiting on the other side of the curtain. This sort of got me thinking about all the amazing things I would have missed out on had I settled for the option of ending my life.

In Christ, I had become a new creature, with a new name, operating in the strength of a heavenly father who had given me life and a renewed sense of purpose. In addition to launching my own publishing company dedicated to helping women authors, I became a published author myself and a columnist for a local newspaper.

With every passing year that was added to my life, God would reveal more and more of the unique plans and purposes that He had for me. Among my great accomplishments is Grounded Jeremiah 29:11, the women's ministry God placed on my heart to establish during the Covid crisis of 2020. Being able to inspire and help other women has been among my greatest joys, and to think, God is not done yet.

The Bible tells us that, "Weeping may endure for a night, but joy comes in the morning." (Psalm 30:5). Even in the darkest of times, we can find solace in knowing that something better is waiting for us on the other side of the curtain. Had my story ended differently, I would not be here to compile this book highlighting the stories of some amazing women. God has a purpose in mind for me and you need to know that He has a purpose in mind for you too.

It's been decades since the mistakes of my youth. The night of my fragility is now but a distant memory tucked away in the corners of my mind. I wake each morning with a smile on my face, proud of the woman I have become.

When I reflect on life before Christ, some days I don't fully understand how I was able to arrive at this place of joy, and self-love. I only know that it was God who had His hand upon me long before the day he saved my life, and because of Christ I now know where I belong.

Some of the most inspirational stories I have ever heard have often been stories that are themed with some element of pain, struggle, or adversity. There may even be some truth to this, but here's what I know to be true. I know that God saved me. Me, an imperfect being with no faith or hope for the future. The person who never felt loved, accepted, or felt like she belonged anywhere. The sinner who had no respect for herself or her body. The mess of a woman who didn't value herself or her own life. God saved m e.

In sharing my story, I hope that others who are faced with similar challenges and feelings of worthlessness will know undoubtedly that Jesus is real. In your darkest hour, know that Jesus is real. When you feel that others have forgotten you, rest assured that Jesus is real. Even if you've made mistakes or sunk so low that it's hard to look up, know with all your heart that Jesus is real.

"For I know the plans I have for you," declares the Lord, "plans to prosper you and not to harm you, plans to give you hope and a future." (Jeremiah 29:11). With a simple whisper of His name and a song of praise in your heart... Jesus has the power to heal, restore, equip, and transport you from a floor in a lonely apartment to a world of hope and endless possibilities... To your defining moment.

Pearls of Wisdom:

1. Our trials and struggles are temporary. By the grace of God, we can endure and make it to the other side.

2. Jesus has the power to heal, restore, and meet you where you are even in the darkest of places.

3. There is no place you can go where God won't be. God knows the beginning and the end and has already made provisions for you.

Dr. Aleta V. Ashford

Dr. Aleta V. Ashford is an author, columnist, and inspirational speaker who has spent most of her career working in the corporate arena. In addition to having completed Business degrees at both the master's and doctoral levels, Dr. Ashford embarked on a second career as a Business Professor where she often included stories in her lectures to make the course lessons more fun and interesting for her students.

After years of serving as an educator and encouraging countless others in the areas of career, business, family, relationships, education, entrepreneurship, and the like. Dr. Ashford took a leap of faith and pursued her dream of becoming a writer. In 2018 she launched Incessant Publishing, LLC, and published her first book "Thirteen Friends To Avoid". This was the start of the Ava Knows brand. Taking this leap of faith not only placed Dr. Ashford on a path to becoming a published author but has also led to multiple speaking engagements.

In addition to her roles as a wife to her husband Gus and a mother to their two sons Brennan and Nicholas, Dr. Ashford is the owner of Incessant Publishing, LLC. She is first and foremost a devoted Christian and the founder of Grounded Jeremiah 29:11, as well as the host of the Grounded Presents podcast, which is now available on iTunes, Spotify, iHeartRadio, and other platforms. Through her books, columns, podcasts, conferences, and ministry, Dr. Ashford has never stopped teaching; her classroom has just gotten a lot bigger.

PURPOSED IN VICTORY

By Sarah Swearingin

"Don't be ashamed of your story, it will one day inspire others." – Unknown

Thinking about this quote really gets me. Like, really gets me. Paraphrased, it means that my story, regardless of what I have walked through—no, what I have overcome—has the power to inspire others.

As I stop to think about this quote, for me personally it rings true. The idea that I can use my journey... a journey of pain, long-suffering, abuse, addiction, codependency, and enabling (you name it, I probably did it) to inspire others. Yes, literally all of what I have been through can be used to represent the glory of God.

My hope is that my story will change the world, or at least someone's world. So that means that your story (Yes, yours!) also has the power to make a difference in somebody's world. The story you are about to read is a story of hope, restoration, and life. My story!!! Above all, it is a story of VICTORY.

For as long as I can remember, addiction was a part of my life. As a kid growing up in the early nineties addiction wasn't something that was widely discussed, nor did I ever really have an awareness of how common it truly was. Yet there I was... On the Mason-Dixon line, growing up in the middle of nowhere. A child impacted by addiction.

Now knowing what I know, I have a better understanding of addiction and how the lives of many others (around the world) have been impacted. As I entered adulthood, addiction would, unfortunately, have an impact on my life as well. Almost as if it was predestined to be a part of my journey. And for a moment, it was.

The odds were stacked against me from the very beginning. For starters, I was a person who had never dealt with my past, my habits, or my hurts. Truth be told, I was carrying the burdens of others including members of my family. In most instances, past hurts from memories that weren't even mine. My life at the time had not yet been given to the Lord, yet I was determined to cling to it (past, present, and future) with everything I had in me.

I was barely eighteen when I graduated from high school and ran 12 hours away from home straight into the arms of a man I had never met. My struggles with addiction would eventually take over my life even though I considered myself to be fully functional. The truth is that I was far from functional. Instead, my lifestyle was crazy and overrun with sex, drugs, and alcohol.

Within a year of settling into my new lifestyle, I would move again. This is where I truly began to lose myself. During this time, if I wasn't drunk, I was high or running amok the city looking for love (any type of love) in literally all the wrong places. By then I had lost all communication with my family and was struggling to maintain a way of life that was completely out of control.

Throughout my early twenties, I would continue to move from place to place. Different places, different men, but unfortunately the same exact routine. By this time, my life was consumed with finding the next man, the next party, and whatever vice I needed to get through the day. I was constantly in search of whatever substance I could get my hands on, and eventually, that substance would become methamphetamine. I didn't know it, but I had officially found the beginning of the end... Crystal meth.

To say that meth had taken control of my life would be an understatement. Meth took over my life and left me homeless, addicted, and running the streets. It had me. Every part of me. Every breath I took through my lungs was a breath in search of my next high. I completely worshiped the ground that this horrendously demonic entity held. It became my god, the idol above all other idols.

Meanwhile, my erratic behavior led to my becoming a person that no one trusted, as well as being declared a thief. Some would even say that I was unlovable and unwanted. Being that I didn't love myself, how could I expect anyone else to love me? Much less God. The way I had chosen to live my life had taken me from couch to couch, man to man, trap house to trap house; and by then I had been in and out of jail and had seen the likes of many judges and courtrooms.

I was headed nowhere fast until one fateful evening that would change my life. It was the night I ended up in jail. This time the judge, whom I had seen many times before, was adamant that he would no longer be seeing me at the level of frequency he had before. I will never forget the stern sound of his voice and the somber look in his eyes when he told me that my fate now rested upon two options:

1. I would be required to get my life together which would include a difficult journey through the court system as well as seeking treatment for my addiction.

2. Go to prison.

It really was that simple. At that moment I didn't know what to do with myself. I was at the end of my rope. All my previous attempts and claims to do better were no longer applicable. My luck (and what some would call grace) had completely run out. In other words, there were no more opportunities to simply try to be better. This was my defining moment.

The devil thought he had me, and in a way, he did. Yet inside, amid all the chaos, I knew with every part of my being that I never wanted to see the inside walls of a prison. So, for me, the choice was obvious. I chose to stand and fight to reclaim my life with the hope of overcoming all the horrible choices I had made.

If I'm being honest, I was scared and clueless about how I would go about getting my life together. Nor did I have any idea what exactly it would entail. I only knew that something needed to happen at that moment, and by the grace of God, something did.

The details of my journey are far too long and intricate to outline in the pages of this book. However, know that the battle was won! GOD fought the battle for me and helped me to overcome my struggles with addiction. He did this... For me! Once I made the choice to climb out of the pit of destruction that had become my life; God cleaned up the mess I had made which is unimaginable being that I barely knew of Him then.

When you look back over your life, are you able to pinpoint a few instances where God too fought your battles? Looking back, were there times when you now realize that God kept the promise that was made in the verses of Deuteronomy? Which is "The Lord your God who goes before you will Himself fight for you, just as He did in Egypt before your eyes." (Deuteronomy 1:30).

If we each think hard, we should all have something to look back on and ponder "How did I ever make it through?" or "How am I even alive?" As I reflect on my own experiences, I am reminded of the lyrics to a song titled "Egypt" by Bethel Worship. "You're the God that fights for me, Lord of every victory, Hallelujah. You have torn apart the sea and led me through the deep, Hallelujah." For me, these words aren't just lyrics. Instead, they represent the story of a battle (my battle) that was fought and won by the grace of God.

An example of a person in the bible who (like me) was at the end of their rope to the point of nearly losing it all was good old' King David, a man after God's own heart. Our Savior's ancestor. When I tell you he struggled, man did David struggle in a major way. Not only was he having an issue with lust, but it was the object of David's obsession that would lead him down the wrong path. The woman's name was Bathsheba.

According to scripture (2 Samuel 11:2), David had seen the woman from afar and from that point on believed that he had to have her. David's desire for Bathsheba was said to be so desperate, that he plotted to have her husband Uriah, who was also David's loyal and trustworthy friend, sent to the front lines of the battlefield, resulting in Uriah's demise (2 Samuel 11:15-17).

Like my battle with addiction, this story outlines the struggles and desires a person can have to fixate on things that they shouldn't and run after them as hard as they can. The struggles I speak of are not just limited to drugs and alcohol. Addiction can come in the form of familiar objects (TVs, cellphones, etc.) and everyday activities (sex, shopping, eating...).

At some point in our lives, we will all struggle with something. Sometimes we even make decisions that we know may get us what we want, though it isn't always what's best for us. The story of David and Bathsheba may have been a dark part of David's journey, but it wasn't the end of his story.

David was confronted by the prophet Nathan (2 Samuel 12), whom God used to change the direction of King David's life. Even as David accepted conviction and was held accountable for his actions as God deemed fit, he was yet forgiven and set free from the bondage of his transgressions. God, in turn, used David's moment of impropriety to change the world!

I love this story, and I hope that others will appreciate it as well. Today, I am a survivor and living witness that God is a God of restoration! Like David, I still had to be held accountable for my actions, but also like David, God took the dark parts of my journey and turned them into something good!

If you are anything like me, I have struggled for most of my life wondering why I am here. Why did I go through all that I went through? The one thing I do know for sure is that God did not have to create us. God wanted to create us. I personally believe that we were created for worship.

Praising God is distinctly outlined in the book of Luke which states "And he answered and said unto them, I tell you that, if these should hold their peace, the stones would immediately cry out." (Luke 19:40). Keeping in mind that

God does not need us to be here to be God. Nor does he need us to tell the world about Him, or even worship Him. Yet—He wants us to praise Him! Therefore, why would we not?!

Imagine, if you will, a beautifully crafted, babbling creek complete with the sound of soft, flowing water moving through the creek bed. The water is so clear that you can see all the way down to the bottom. In fact, it's the clearest water you have ever seen. So clear that you can see what appears to be an infinite number of stones of all shapes, colors, and sizes.

Now imagine if we as God's creation ceased to worship Him. According to His word, the very rocks (including the millions at the bottom of our babbling creek bed) will cry out to worship the Lord! Imagine all the stones in the world worshipping God. That would be the only sound we would ever hear. Now if a stone can worship God, aren't we as humans capable of doing that much more?

Our commitment to God isn't just limited to our worship of Him, it includes the relationship that comes from knowing Him. Our connection with God should be reflected in our homes, our jobs, and the relationships and connections that we have with other people.

As Christians, we should be moving about our lives in a way that reflects the Lord, fully knowing that He is an ever-present God who is with us as we live and serve. Most importantly we want those who do not know the Lord as their Savior to see the good in us, and not question the goodness of God based on our behavior.

As I write these words, I want it to be known that I struggle in each of these areas. We all do! The reality is that homes aren't always perfect, and our connections with others won't always be harmonious. The point is our lives are a journey to sanctification, of which the purpose is in the goal.

At the beginning of this chapter, I spoke a lot about addiction and the impact it had on my life before transitioning to our purpose in Christ. By now you're probably wondering, what do all these factors have to do with each other? Allow me to explain.

Addiction nearly stole my life and almost robbed me of my purpose. Praise the Lord! I no longer live in the bondage of addiction, as Jesus erased all of it when I accepted Him into my heart. God removed it all and used it for His glory! The issues that once plagued me are now my testimony. I can move forward in Christ toward the prize of eternal life and so can you!

Even if you are someone who has never dealt with an addiction, try replacing that word with whatever stronghold you have ever had to overcome or will overcome by filling in the blanks and making your own declarations!

_____ tried to steal my life from me.

_____ tried to steal my purpose.

_____ tried to steal my joy.

Since overcoming my addiction, my purpose in this world is to ensure that others know about this amazing figure that I have in my life. That of whom I speak of my friend is God. God who created the heavens and the earth, the zillions of rocks, the stars in the sky, the beautiful flowers in the meadow, the birds in the air... God.

God created all of this with me in mind, and you in mind! Better yet, He knew that this world needed you in it. More specifically, this world needs you to find your purpose and worship in glorifying God. If you don't already have a relationship with God, you do have a choice.

The gift of salvation is free and something that God gives us all a choice to receive. If you do not know Jesus as your personal Lord and Savior, I implore you to pray this prayer with all your heart, believe, and allow the heavens to rejoice that you have chosen to be a child of God. It really is that simple!

Jesus, thank you, Lord. Thank you for loving me and thank you for your death and resurrection on the cross for my sins. You did it so I could have everlasting life, and I declare you my Lord and Savior forever and ever. Thank you, Lord, for forgiving me. I accept you as my Lord and Savior. Please come and live in my heart! I love you Jesus. A men.

Congratulations! You found Him! Angels are rejoicing because you have found your purpose! You now are a member of the family of Jesus! I am so proud of you! The women who are featured throughout this book are proud of you as well. Most of all, Jesus is extremely proud and excited that you have made this decision. He loves you and is rejoicing in the streets of heaven at this very moment.

As this chapter comes to a close, I want you to know that you are a precious jewel in the eyes of our Lord. Isn't it comforting to know that no matter what we have done, God loves us, forgives us, and has the power to restore us? He created us with a purpose in mind and has a special and unique plan for each of us! Even in the sin of addiction, God loves you, He is proud of you, and He desires you. This is exactly what it means to experience unconditional l ove.

Pearls of Wisdom:

1. The curse of addiction is real, but the Lord has overcome all, and it does not have the be the end of your story.

2. Your life has a purpose, and the Lord has created you for it! The world needs you to find your purpose.

3. God has the power to take the worst parts of our story and use it for his glory according to His purpose.

Sarah Swearingin

Sarah Swearingin currently resides in southwest Missouri where she has lived for the past decade. She has been happily married to Michael since 2019, and they have two children, Jaycee and Kaden. In her free time, Sarah enjoys gardening, and spending time with her family and friends, as well as occasionally going to a good baseball game or t wo.

In 2014 Sarah rededicated her life to the Lord and has been working to serve diligently ever since. Leading up to the Grounded book anthology, through the prodding and leading of the Holy Spirit, Sarah took a leap of faith and launched Thrive, Living Free Ministries. Thrive Living Free is an outreach ministry that uses small group-based principles and relationships to share the love and freedom that Jesus provides.

Through her service, Sarah hopes to be able to share the redemptive love of Jesus with the world, as God allows! She is also an advocate for those struggling with substance abuse and addiction, life-controlling issues, and homelessness, partnering with neighboring ministries and alliances around the nation!

Joining the Grounded Jeremiah 29:11 platform in 2021 was an exciting moment in Sarah's life. Since then, she has continued in her support of Grounded Jeremiah 29:11 and is looking forward to future collaborations beyond the anthology project.

GOD HAS THE FINAL SAY

By Gwendolyn Mann

We all go through trials and struggles as Christians, and there are times when our faith will be tested. I can only tell you that God has been faithful to me. He has saved me time after time, forgiven me, and loved me endlessly even when I didn't deserve it. God has always shown me grace, mercy, and everlasting love. This chapter of my life is no exception.

My journey starts on a day that I had been anticipating for so long, surgery day. The day that all my pain would go away. The moment when my body would be normal again. At least from what I was told. I longed to function at 100 percent and for pain medications and injections to be a thing of the past. My back would finally be healed, I would reclaim my life, and it would all start with the long waited, highly anticipated, "Lord, I thank you in advance", surgery day.

When I arrived at the hospital the morning of the surgery I was prepped and ready for a procedure that was estimated to take a few hours. For the most part, things had gone according to plan up until my time in the operating room. The surgery was already in progress when there was a loud "BOOM" and then all the lights went out.

The surgery had not gone according to plan. The procedure which should have taken a few hours took an unexpected turn and was recategorized as an incomplete surgery that took as much as five hours. It was beyond anything I could have ever imagined. Five hours in an operating room and I still needed another surgery.

Confined to a hospital bed and in agonizing pain, I was hospitalized for three days before being transferred to another facility to have the surgery completed. This was not at all the outcome I had envisioned. By this point I should have been home, recovering, and well on my way to becoming pain-free. Yet, there I was. Anticipating yet another surgery, as my hope and certainty surrounding my healing was slowly diminishing by the minute.

Waiting for the surgery was a real test of my faith. It was during this time that I began to lose hope and question

God. Why my surgery? Why was this happening to me? Even as a Christian who (under normal circumstances) is deeply rooted in my faith; I had become so anxious and fixated on the pain, that it had become increasingly difficult to trust God at that moment. Instead, I found myself listening intently to the medical professionals and putting my trust solely into man, forgetting momentarily that it is ultimately God who heals and can fix all things.

As believers, it is a normal part of our culture and dialog to profess our faith and belief that God is a healer and deliverer for those who love Him. However, in times of trouble, how likely are we as Christians to believe it? Putting our total faith in God is something that is easier said than done and requires much patience and practice. The real test of our faith as Christians is when things aren't working in our favor and amid our pain and suffering.

According to Psalm 118:8, "It is better to trust in the Lord than to put confidence in man." Again, it's easy to trust God when things are going well. However, even when life becomes unbearable, we should still seek to maintain our faith. Here I had been hanging on every word of my doctors when it is God who guides the hands of the doctors!

Remember in all things God has the final say. As children of God, we can walk in the fullness of knowing that God does not lie. Nor will he leave us or forsake us. Though the details of my medical diagnosis appeared bleak and my future uncertain; God is truly the one who has the power to intercede and bring forth the healing that I was seeking. Though I had no idea what the future would hold for me, I knew from that moment on that I would trust God.

The more time progressed, the worse my condition became. Even after the second procedure, I was still in pain and by then needed a home nurse and total care. My family also shared the responsibility of caring for me, and I can recall feeling nervous and scared about the fact that I was no longer able to do some of the things I could do before the surgeries. Yet, in my struggles, I continued to trust God.

The final procedure left a large wound on my back that required cleaning and for the dressings to be changed regularly. One day while dressing the wound, one of my caregivers noticed some abnormalities. After a visit to the doctor's office, it was confirmed that the wound had indeed become infected. Even then, I continued to trust God.

This latest prognosis required additional surgery to fight the infection in my back. Hearing the news of a new surgery was like being hit with a ton of bricks as it had taken every ounce of strength I had just to make it to this point. Even then, more than ever before, I still trusted God.

The additional surgery did not result in the outcome I expected. Stressed and disappointed, I did my best to remain hopeful. Though the news wasn't good, inside I knew that I had to keep pushing, if for no other reason but for my children and grandchildren. I also knew that the path toward getting better would require a total shift in my mindset.

The part of my story where I truly had to channel my faith and trust in God was when the final of the three surgeries led to my being placed in a rehabilitation center to recover. Determined to go home a healed person, on the days when my faith was tested I prayed and asked God to provide me with the strength I needed to heal.

There were days when I felt discouraged and moments when the pain was so unbearable that I could hardly think straight. I had to learn how to walk again and coming to the realization that my healing would now take longer than initially planned left me depressed and wondering where I would find the faith and strength to make it through.

Even as it shriveled to the size of a tiny mustard seed, it's no secret where I found my faith. I found faith and courage in Jesus Christ. Deuteronomy 31:6 encourages us to "Be strong and of good courage, do not fear nor be afraid of them; for the Lord your God, he is the one who goes with you. He will not leave you nor forsake you." In my darkest hour, my heavenly father showed up once again to remind me whose daughter I was and answered my prayers with strength like no other.

Even as I doubted Him, God filled my fragile spirit with hope at a time when I didn't have any. Though Rehabilitation therapy was painful and hard, God renewed my faith and gave me the strength to keep fighting for my life, myself, and my family. Because of Christ, I was able to defeat the enemy and win more battles than I can outline in a single chapter.

There is not a day that goes by that I don't praise God for restoring my health. Just as He had done my entire life, God showed up once again to remind me who He is and never left me. Instead, He saved me and allowed me to share my story, and it is never far from my mind that my journey could have ended far differently had God not interceded on my behalf.

By sharing my story, I want others to know that God keeps His promises. Regardless of your circumstances, never be afraid to call on God, especially during times when you feel that you don't have the courage or strength to carry on. You can always call on God and ask Him to give you what you need to move forward. It was during one of the lowest points of my life that He healed, gave me a powerful testimony, and allowed me to come out on top. What He did for me, He can surely do for you too.

If by chance you don't know God, I hope my testimony introduces you to Him. My prayer is that He gives you the strength you need to face any obstacle, hope that the storm will pass, and the courage to defeat the enemy. God bless you and keep you. Most importantly and in all things, God has the final say.

Pearls of Wisdom

1. Trust in the Lord even when things become unbearable. With God, all things are possible (Matthew 19:26)

2. Remember that God will remain with us even through trying times. Don't be afraid to ask Him for what you need.

3. God guides the hands of doctors and has the final say when it comes to our healing and restoration.

Gwendolyn Mann

Gwendolyn Mann is a former employee and retiree of the Georgia Department of Corrections and currently serves in the role of Director on the board of her local Chamber of Commerce. Gwendolyn and her husband Marvin are residents of Glenwood, Georgia where they are the proud owners of Divine Inspirations Café. Together they have six children, seventeen grandchildren, and three great-grandchildren all of whom they are very proud. In her spare time, Gwendolyn enjoys reading, watching a good movie, and spending time with her husband and family.

Gwendolyn Mann is first and foremost a woman of God and a proud member of Mt. Moriah Baptist Church in Higgston, Georgia, where she serves faithfully under the leadership of Pastor, Bishop A. Tim Chatman and his lovely wife, First Lady Rev. Verlinda Chatman.

Gwendolyn is also the aunt of Dr. Aleta V. Ashford (founder of Grounded Jeremiah 29:11) and was present at her first book signing several years ago. Gwendolyn, who is a first-time author, is honored to be a part of the Grounded book anthology and hopes that her story inspires others.

YOUR STORY IS GOD'S GLORY

By Min. Sherilla Pittman

Your story is God's glory. It took me a while to grasp this revelation but once I did, it became a lifeline that would bring me hope no matter what I had to face in life. In sharing my story, my prayer is that you too will find hope in the most difficult of times. Though our struggles may be different, the one thing that unifies us is that we all have a story.

We are all unique creatures with different paths in life. Understand that every part of our life has been orchestrated for a divine purpose for which God has worked things out for our good. The individual paths that we travel in life, whether by choice, chance, or even those that are imposed upon us; are the substance of who we are. What one person has endured, perhaps another person would not be able to bear; and what may have worked in other circumstances, may not work for you. Regardless of how you arrived at this point in your life, you need to know that your story is God's glory, and somebody is waiting to hear it.

Reflecting on my life as a child, I can honestly say that I had a drug problem. I had a mother who drug me to church, drug me to bible study, Sunday school, and choir rehearsal. By now you get the picture. It was during this time that I developed a love for the bible. Its stories of drama, defeat, triumph, and miracles can be read repeatedly with fresh perspectives each time.

Though I was always in church, it is important to note that the church wasn't always in me. Back then if someone would have said "Now that's not fair to a child. Children should play and enjoy their childhood." I would have been among the first to agree as I never understood why all my friends were hanging out and having fun while I had to be in church. However, what I didn't know back then that I know now is that every aspect of my life, especially my childhood, is a part of God's intricate plan.

The word of God is living, breathing, full of power, and effective in transforming us into instruments for His purpose. As stated in the book of Hebrews, "For the word of God is alive and active. Sharper than any double-edged sword, it penetrates even to dividing soul and spirit, joints, and marrow; it judges the thoughts and attitudes of the heart. Nothing in all creation is hidden from God's sight. Everything is uncovered and laid bare before the eyes of him to whom we must give account." (Hebrews 4:12-13). What book, if any, could compare to that?

I was around the tender age of nine when I read the bible and came across the suffering of Jesus. As a child, it was hard to understand the torture, ridicule, and humiliation that was inflicted upon someone who had done nothing that would warrant hairs being ripped from his beard, much less the crown of thorns that had been purposely pushed into his head to cause more of his blood to flow.

Instantly I was overwhelmed with sorrow. Tears ran down my face as the sheer essence of evil in the heart of man had become so clear to me. I can remember thinking to myself, "How could they be so evil and so mean?" It was then that I first heard a voice within answer "You fight with your sisters, you disobey your mom, and you tell lies. Evil is evil." I knew at that moment that I wanted to follow Jesus.

It was then that I asked Jesus to come into my heart, wash me of my sinful and evil nature, and take my life into his hands. Hearing the story of Jesus, who was humble, innocent, and had suffered on my behalf; was the catalyst that led to my being baptized. Little did I understand as a child that becoming a follower of Jesus Christ doesn't make us exempt from the pain and suffering of this world.

Soon, after my baptism, it started. The inappropriate touching. Things being done to me as a child that was difficult to understand. Things that made me feel confused and shameful inside. How could I even begin to put it into words when at the time I didn't even know what it was?

Whatever "it" was, it conjured feelings of hopelessness and guilt. As I would soon learn, there was a certain amount of guilt that came along with being told things like "If you tell, the family won't believe you...They'll be mad at you...This will break up the family..." Though I didn't understand it, what I did understand was that I was harboring a painful secret.

It was a heavy burden for a child to carry with so many unanswered questions like, "Why me? Why is this happening? What's wrong with me? Is this normal?" It was a confusing time in my life in which seeds of fear and self-doubt had been planted within me by a person who was supposed to love and protect me. As a child of God, how could this happen?

As an adult, I now have a better understanding of the enemy and who he is. The enemy who is often described as being the most subtle of all creatures lurks about to see whom he can destroy. This includes our children, particularly those who are young and innocent.

It is my personal belief that the enemy launches his attacks on children (as young as possible) to thwart the plan that God has for their lives before they are even old enough to discern what's happening to them.

Though I may not have understood much at the time, inside I knew that this thing that was happening to me was pure evil. Perhaps it was the correlation of shame, and secrecy, coupled with the fact that these experiences evoked similar feelings and emotions that I had often felt when reading about the suffering of Jesus Christ. These emotions were among the first indicators alerting my innocent spirit that something was terribly wrong.

Though the abuse didn't end right away, I survived by gravitating more toward Jesus. I prayed often and read the bible where I found example after example of others who had struggled and survived insurmountable sufferings all by the grace and goodness of God. These stories filled my spirit with the hope that I too would survive and overcome. It wasn't long before I began praising God for giving me the strength to endure, and proclaimed His goodness to anyone who would listen.

It wasn't long before friends, and others around the neighborhood started attending church services and getting baptized. As I grew stronger in my faith, I started praying for my abuser asking God to remove the turmoil from within them. I had no way of knowing that my first act of intercession would be interceding for the person who was causing me harm.

The effects of the trauma from my childhood followed me well into my adulthood. By now you may even be wondering, "How can a tragic story about abuse, be worked out for a person's good?" That's a great question. Let's start with the most obvious. There's nothing good about abuse or the egregious act that occurred in my childhood. No child should ever have to experience something like this.

The trauma I suffered at the hands of my abuser is something that stayed with me for a long time and has affected me in indescribable ways. However, it is also important to note that all our experiences, including those that are good and bad, help to shape us and contribute to our becoming who we are.

God created us all with a purpose in mind. If the enemy can divert our attention towards focusing on our hurts, and disappointments, or spending an endless amount of time trying to figure out what happened, why it happened, or the person or persons who should be blamed for our circumstances; This leads to less time for us to focus on more important things like our salvation and our purpose in life.

As a victim of trauma and abuse, at some point in my life, I had a choice to make. Either I could continue to dwell over the atrocities that had occurred and maintain the feelings of bitterness and resentment that were brewing on the inside; or I could fight for my healing, reclaim my life, and push toward the mark of discovering the purpose of my existence.

Fixating on the past can lead to strongholds that hold us in bondage and hinder us from reaching our God-given destiny. This is not to say that we are not impacted by the things that happen in our lives. Instead, it's a testament that we must be vigilant in discerning when it is the work of the enemy. The same enemy who seeks to deceive, destroy, and would like for us all to believe he doesn't exist.

Imagine a puppeteer holding the strings of a marionette. Puppeteers are masters at creating narratives and illusions and are skillful at controlling the strings of their puppets. Now imagine that the marionette is an abuser and that the puppet master controlling the strings is the enemy. The puppet master can control the abuser's movement and actions because the abuser is in bondage to the enemy.

However, as a child of the Most High you my friend are not!

You are not bound by the snares or "strings" of the enemy. You may have suffered or been victimized but you don't have to remain a victim. You are a victor! You are free to move beyond the sins of your past and free to choose whether you will push past the hurt to reclaim your life. Alternatively, you also have the option to dwell in the past and continue to allow the enemy to pull the strings attached to your emotions, self-esteem, and overall well-being.

Redemption may be a painful process, but it starts with your moving forward toward your victory. The first steps aren't always easy and may involve you putting some space between yourself and the problem, or perhaps even seeking support or counseling. Regardless of the route you choose to take, always remember that you are a survivor. You are still here. You survived and made it through by the grace of God. Therefore, don't allow yourself to reside in a place that God has already delivered you from.

The defining moment in my life as a believer was when I truly came to know that God is working things out for my good. Take a moment here, I mean really take a moment to look back and think about all things that have transpired in your life up to this point. The victories and the failures.

Not only was God working everything out, but He has also been moving you toward a purpose that is greater than you!

I close my story with a special message of hope for victims of abuse. Whether the abuse was verbal, emotional, physical, sexual, or even a form of substance abuse; My message of hope for you is that you no longer have to be a victim. You have a choice! You can choose to be in bondage, or you can choose to be victorious. Just know that in everything you've been through, God is still operating on your behalf. God has a plan for you therefore get stronger! Get wiser! Find freedom in Him! Not just for you and your life, but for the lives of those around you. Your story is God's glory.

Pearls of Wisdom:

1. Somebody is waiting to hear your story. Don't be afraid to share your journey with others as it may be a bridge to their deliverance.

2. Without process, there is no progress. Your purpose is waiting for you. Don't be afraid to move forward.

3. The Choice is Yours. Choose to move toward your victory and the things that God has designed for you.

Minister Sherilla Pittman

Minister Sherilla Pittman is a native of Kansas who received her Christian calling at a young age and has served in various areas of ministry for many years.

Min. Pittman holds a bachelor's degree in management and attended The Spectrum School of Ministry in New Port Richey, FL, and Life Christian University in Lutz, FL. She is a licensed and ordained, Elder serving on the Ministerial Alliance Team at Deliverance Tabernacle Christian Center in Pensacola, FL.

Minister Pittman is a motivational speaker and leader of the Transformers Women Group in Pensacola. She has also served as Program Director for the Hopeville Community Development Corporation a non-profit transitional facility, where she mentored and coached women coming out of prison and overcoming the chains of addiction and abuse.

A loving mother, grandmother, and wife of 29 years, Minister Pittman has a willing heart and desire to see people transformed by the renewal of their minds; and is committed to service and being one of the many yielded vessels God uses to manifest His glory in the earth.

BEAUTIFULLY BROKEN WARRIOR

By Vanessa Kortz

M y story begins with one of my favorite quotes by Carly Simon which reads, "A really strong woman accepts the war she went through and is ennobled by her scars." This quote hits home for me as it symbolizes the many different struggles, I have had to endure throughout my life.

For as long as I can remember I have struggled with low confidence and self-love. As far back as middle school, I have wrestled with issues concerning my body image and self-esteem to the degree of sometimes starving myself or causing myself to vomit after a meal. There were days when I prayed to God for a body that was different from the one that I had. The fact that I had no friends didn't help. I was pretty much a loner, who often walked around feeling ashamed and embarrassed. Never revealing to anyone the details of the constant battle I was facing inside.

My issues continued throughout middle school and worsened by the time I entered high school. Even after having participated in activities like cheerleading and the drill team; I would often feel uncomfortable about my size and weight which was about 120 pounds at the time. The pressure to look a certain way was overwhelming and had overshadowed every aspect of my life. Well, every aspect except one.

It was at church that I discovered my love of singing. Singing in the choir gave me a peace that I had never known. For the most part, I felt loved and accepted by members of the church. However, this would soon change shortly after I graduated and became pregnant with my first child. In addition to being treated differently by people who were supposed to love me; I was shunned by members of the church congregation to the degree that I stopped singing and attending church services altogether.

Though I was thankful for my son and the gift of becoming a mother, my battle with low self-esteem is something that would follow me well into my adult life, especially in my relationships with men. One failed relationship after another, I never fully felt like I measured up. Broken inside, I started on a downward spiral that created a pattern of my settling for less than what I deserved.

Unfortunately, no one would suffer more from my poor decisions during this phase of my life than my son. My need for attention and acceptance coupled with excessive drinking led to my losing all control and neglecting pertinent parts of his childhood. I would go on to abandon my son for the first man who showed me attention and before I knew it, I had moved to a new city with a man I barely knew.

There I was in a new place where I had no family or no one to turn to for help as I would soon learn when the abuse started. I will never forget the sting of being slapped in my face. Much less the fear of realizing that I was alone, and a long way away from home.

It wasn't long before I found out I was pregnant again. A kick here, a slap there, and several violent arguments later I suffered a miscarriage. It was one of the lowest points of my life where I was left feeling like I had failed to protect another child of mine. A child who never had the chance to enter this world.

I hadn't prayed in years, but it was then that I began to cry out to God for strength and guidance. For a while, the beatings stopped, and things were good. Yet by the time I found out I was pregnant with my second child, the abuse had resumed and escalated to impromptu trips to the emergency room where I often found myself coming up with elaborate stories to explain my injuries. As painful as the stitches and staples were, the effects of the emotional abuse lasted much longer.

To this day I'm not sure why I stayed as long as I did. Instead of leaving I found myself settling for daily dosages of abuse, infidelity, and neglect. By the grace of God, I gave birth to a healthy baby boy, and for the first time in my life, I was determined to turn my life around.

Whether it was verbal or physical abuse, my circumstances remained the same. Once again, I cried out to God and prayed for deliverance for myself and my son. Over time God gave me the strength and courage to fight back and eventually freed me in an unexpected way.

My deliverance from the abuse may not have happened the way that I expected it to happen, however, I fully believe that there are no accidents in life. God had orchestrated my safety and freedom and had done so in such a way that I would have to rely solely upon Him. For the first time in my life, I was incarcerated for six months.

Adjusting to my new life was hard. Though my circumstances were temporary, contemplating my future from a jail cell often left me with an overwhelming sense of fear and anxiety. I felt lost and completely out of my element. Not to mention being consumed with the worry of not knowing where my child was or if he was okay.

I cried quietly in my bed every night and wasn't sure how I was going to survive such a dark and painful reality. Even in what could very well have been classified as the most desolate time in my life, God still showed mercy and grace in meeting me where I was.

Two weeks after my arrival, I received a bible from a woman who had heard my cries and was kind enough to pray with me. From that moment on I began studying, praying regularly, and seeking God for guidance amid my circumstances. Slowly but surely, I was learning to put my trust in God and even established a morning routine for myself that included getting down on my knees to pray.

It wasn't long before other female detainees started kneeling beside me to pray as a part of their morning routine. Soon after, I was asked by some of the women to lead a small bible study group. My little routine had now turned into a support group where we studied the word and engaged in meaningful discussions about life and the issues we were facing. As a result, some of the ladies were even led to Christ.

Through the experience of helping other women, I was truly able to find myself and began to understand my purpose for being there. Though I wasn't sure what would become of my life after my time in lock-up, I knew that I would be going home a different woman. A woman who was saved, more confident, and determined to find her sons and reunite with her family.

The day that I was released, I was informed that someone was waiting to pick me up which was strange considering I hadn't talked to anyone for quite some time. When I walked outside and saw my father standing there, I knew that there was a God. The feeling of seeing my father at that moment is unspeakable. Like the unconditional love of our heavenly father, seeing my father was a reminder that there was no mistake that I could make that would separate me from his love.

The process of getting my children back was not without incident but in the end, God is a loving and merciful God who saw it fit to deliver me from the clutches of bondage, and by His grace, I was reunited with both of my children, and my relationship with my family was restored. I went on to get my life back and God sent me a new love to help me raise my boys as well as a little bundle of joy that we created together.

I have faced a lot of battles in my life. I've been battered, bruised, and broken. The path to loving myself and discovering my worth has not been an easy one. Yet as I look back and reflect on every trial and struggle, I can attest with great certainty that I was never alone. God was holding my hand and giving me the strength and courage, I needed to stand and fight.

God saved me and gave me a new sense of purpose. As a survivor, I now know that hitting rock bottom wasn't the end of my story. Instead, it was a defining moment in my life and the start of my journey toward helping others who are suffering from abuse and domestic violence.

Where I was once broken and riddled with low self-esteem and self-doubt. I stand proudly today as a warrior. A beautiful warrior, broken no more. In sharing my story my prayer is for other women to know that God is able and willing to intercede and deliver you from the depths of even the darkest of places if you trust Him. Regardless of your circumstances or the path you choose to take in life; never forget that you too are a warrior. A beautiful warrior. Free. Delivered. Broken no more.

Pearls of Wisdom:

1. God is a loving God who has the power to turn things around for your good.

2. God can heal you and deliver you from the depths of even the darkest of places.

3. There is no mistake that you could make that is terrible enough to separate you from the love of Jesus.

Vanessa Kortz

Vanessa Kortz is a domestic abuse survivor who has devoted her time to helping women in similar situations. Throughout her journey, she has overcome a series of challenges that led her back to Christ and made her the strong woman she is today.

In addition to being the mother of three children of her own, Vanessa is also a bonus mom to two girls of whom she has been blessed to watch grow and help to become independent, mighty women of God. Vanessa is married to the man of her dreams. The man that God handpicked for her when her life was upside down with no sense of direction. The man who helped her to see that she was beautiful inside and out and showed her what it's like to truly be loved and appreciated.

Together, Vanessa and her husband have built a life based on the notion, "We were born for greatness and as long as we work as a team we can and will achieve all of our dreams!" Vanessa currently resides in Texas and is the founder of Rise Up, a ministry she started to support other women.

BEYOND THE SURFACE

By Tonia F. Walker-Singleton

T o the rest of the world, I had it all together. I was a wife, mother, full-time employee, part-time student, ordained minister, and founder of a nonprofit organization. However, beyond the surface, I was suffering in silence and living with a painful secret.

Years ago, I was living what I thought to be a normal life. Though I was struggling with chronic pain and migraines, I somehow managed to serve in the church while volunteering and helping the homeless and less fortunate in my local community. During this time, I experienced good days and bad days, but seldom would anyone ever hear me complain. If not for some unforeseen changes at work, I would likely have continued to maintain the facade.

At the time I was working for a company that was undergoing significant changes, including layoffs. Unfortunately, the fast-paced environment caused stress levels to soar, and the overall atmosphere grew burdensome. Although I wasn't overly concerned about being laid off myself, the thought did cross my mind and gave me cause for concern. Despite my best efforts to encourage my coworkers to stay positive, I eventually realized that the constant murmuring and complaints were starting to take a toll on my mental state.

Outside of work, the church ministry was also changing and reassessing its goals, which made it difficult to communicate the message I felt God had placed on my heart. The more difficult my circumstances became, the more challenging it was to focus. Mentally I wasn't as sharp as I had been, and even when I attempted to rest and close my eyes my mind was always racing with a perpetual play-by-play from the events of the day. I was exhausted. As much as I wanted to pretend that everything was okay, the issues I was facing with my overall health and well-being were intensifying to a level that could no longer be ignored.

While the mental and physical challenges I faced were agonizing, the real tragedy is the number of years I spent ignoring the symptoms and neglecting to seek professional help. Instead, I went about my daily life with an optimistic persona, but beyond the surface, I was overrun with chronic pain, debilitating migraines, and severe depression and anxiety. All this, while maintaining a pleasant disposition; determined to be a beacon of hope for others in their time of darkness.

Dealing with illness can be challenging, particularly when it comes to mental health issues. The associated stigma can be particularly difficult to manage, especially within the African American community where seeking professional help is often viewed as being taboo.

Even as believers, how often are we encouraged to "take our burdens to the Lord in prayer" and simply leave them there? More times than not, I had conditioned myself to do just that. Little did I know that God had different plans and was about to intervene in a major way.

For years, I had accepted panic attacks, anxiety, and heart palpitations as a normal part of my life. It was just another day at work, the day when I suddenly started experiencing chest tightness, heart palpitations, nausea, and migraines at a level that I had never experienced before. Everything was spinning around me, and before I knew it, I was being rushed to the hospital.

In a matter of minutes, my entire world changed. I was at a point in my journey where I finally realized that relying solely on my own abilities wasn't enough. I needed to let go of my pride, preconceived thoughts, ideas, and plans; and come to terms with the fact that I couldn't fully comprehend God's plan. Trusting God required me to acknowledge that some things were beyond my control. By placing my faith in the Lord, I found a firm belief and assurance.

Numbers 23:19, declares, "God is not a man that He should lie, neither the son of man, that He should repent. Hath He said, and will He not do it? Or hath He spoken, and will He not make it good."

Believing in God comes naturally when everything seems to be going great – when there's enough money in your bank account, food in the pantry, and bills paid on time. But what if you're struggling to make ends meet, with no money in the bank, no food in the cupboard, and no means to pay your bills? How can you trust in God when you're ill and everything around you seems to be falling apart?

I remember it like it was yesterday. That was the day when I heard the voice of God say to me clearly, "It doesn't matter what it feels like, it doesn't matter what your situation looks like, it doesn't matter what it sounds like. Trust me. Do not focus your eyesight on your situation, rather focus on the one who can help you overcome your situation."

It is by the grace of God that my condition wasn't as severe as a heart attack or stroke, yet life-altering no less. I was officially diagnosed with depression. An illness that often made me feel like I was in a dark cave and couldn't escape. An illness that I was too embarrassed to tell anyone about. An illness that even after it was suggested that I seek the support of a licensed therapist or psychiatrist; I can remember thinking "There is no way in the world that I am going to see a psychiatrist or therapist." Though it took some time, eventually I saw both.

Life can be challenging, and I've certainly had my share of bad days. But through it all, I always strive to make the most of every day because I have come to understand how precious life is. I still have scars. However, I no longer allow my circumstances to hold me back. Instead, I choose to see myself as a strong, resilient woman, refined and polished by God's grace.

My faith has taught me to trust God amid difficult situations, even when others don't understand my journey. As long as I know that I am worthy in God's eyes, it is worth the sacrifice. Today I'm no longer hindered by the opinions of others. Nor do I feel shame or embarrassment when it comes to seeking professional help. I now realize that therapy is man's medical intervention that God used to heal me. Though it is God who will make me whole.

While I still suffer from debilitating migraines and other health issues, I am no longer depressed. Hallelujah! When faced with difficult situations, I didn't always comprehend everything that was happening. Nevertheless, I placed my trust in the Lord. Just as I had done countless times in the past knowing that He would see me through. Without fail, God always came through for me.

"He that dwelleth in the secret place of the most High shall abide under the shadow of the Almighty, I will say of the Lord, He is my refuge and my fortress: my God; in Him will I trust." Psalm 91:1-2.

When you start living beyond the surface, there are those who may not understand your journey and may even abandon you when you don't measure up to their expectations. However, it's important to remember that God will never leave you or forsake you. For this reason, you can confidently move forward, never giving up no matter the obstacles or pitfalls that come your way.

Pearls of Wisdom:

1. Regardless of what you are going through, God has the power to heal and make you whole.

2. When it comes to your mental health, physical health, and emotional well-being, never be afraid to seek professional help.

3. Others may not understand your journey. Trust God and never give up despite the obstacles and pitfalls that come your way.

Tonia F. Walker-Singleton

Tonia F. Walker-Singleton is a wife and proud mother of two adult children. During her career, she served as a customer service representative for Time Inc. for 30 years, where she held various positions including her role as a Consumer Affairs Representative. Apart from her professional experience, Mrs. Walker-Singleton has a strong record of serving local nonprofits and religious organizations in the Tampa Bay community. In 2006, she earned an Associate of Science Degree in Office Management Technology, and in 2008, she obtained a Certificate in Business Administration, from Hillsborough Community College in Tampa, Florida.

Mrs. Walker-Singleton has been actively involved in the church since her teenage years. Her passion for helping others began with a small act of kindness, providing school supplies for her nieces and nephews. Today, the small act of collecting school supplies for her family members has blossomed into Beauty of a Woman Ministry, Inc., a nonprofit ministry that she founded in 2008 and incorporated in March 2012.

An Ordained Evangelist, Mrs. Walker-Singleton is also a self-published author of two books: Transforming into God's Beautiful Butterfly: Uncovering Your Inner Beauty and My Identity Crisis: The Transformation Process. Her books are available on all major outlets.

A SONG IN MY HEART

By Nicole L. Crawford

I can remember growing up as an only child and spending a lot of time alone. One of the things I would do to keep myself occupied was create little songs about whatever I was thinking about or playing with at the time. At any given time, I had a million melodies just floating in my head. My ultimate dream was to be a singer. Though I never really thought that singing would be a skill that I could develop, I would soon learn that God had other plans.

I was a young married woman with a small child the day that God dropped a song in my heart. One day while washing dishes and daydreaming as I stared out of a window, God placed the most amazing tune in my spirit. I can recall being so excited, I thought it was the best song I had ever heard. Once I found the courage to share it with my husband, he encouraged me to write down the lyrics and even helped me to produce it.

Throughout my journey, God has always had a way of providing for me when I least expected it. This time was no exception. I was fortunate to have married into a musical family and blessed to have a husband who would become an integral part of my development as a singer and songwriter. This was the moment I realized that God had already given me exactly what I needed long before I ever knew I needed it.

After the song was produced, I wasn't quite sure what exactly it was that I was supposed to be doing. Was I to pursue some type of singing career? At the time, I had no idea. This was one of the most difficult and uncomfortable times of my life. With all the uncertainty surrounding my next move, I began to pray and ask God for guidance.

The path to pursuing music was uncertain and extremely scary for me. Therefore, when I prayed, I prayed specifically. I was intentional concerning the things I asked for as I was seeking a clear and direct answer from the Lord. "Lord, if I'm supposed to sing, I need you to reveal it to me at a church where I am not a parishioner, via a message from a pastor who isn't my pastor, and on a day that isn't Sunday." This was my prayer, which could not have been any more specific than that.

Several months later, on a Tuesday evening, I attended a church service with my husband who was playing bass guitar at an outdoor revival for his aunt's church. Tired from working that day, I did not feel up to going but wanted to support my husband. I was able to find a less conspicuous spot in the back and had just settled into my seat when I was approached by the pastor. "You sing, don't you?" she asked. I felt completely exposed, yet hesitantly replied, "Yes".

"I know because God told me you do." She responded. Tears immediately began to roll down my cheeks. To be honest I don't remember much that was said following the realization that God had just answered my prayer with the exact specifications I had asked for.

In that one moment, so many things became real for me. Not that I didn't trust God before, but now I had just experienced firsthand that God is real, and He loves me. He listens to me. He heard my prayer and he answered. This was all the evidence and proof that I would ever need to be fully committed to Christ.

There I was. I had finally received the answer to my prayer but what did it even mean? I clearly understood that I had an assignment, however, was not so clear on how I would go about pursuing my desire to sing. According to James 2:17 "In the same way, faith by itself, if it is not accompanied by action, is dead." Now that I had received the answer to my prayer, I knew that it was time for me to step out on faith and expand myself musically. This was the start of my musical journey.

Starting out I had no idea where God wanted me to be, not to mention I had no real confidence in my voice, my gift, or my musical ability. I was scared. Once again God would show up to meet me where I was. Before I knew it, my family and I were attending a church where we all served on the praise team together. My husband played the bass guitar, my daughter played the drums, and my son played the congas. In addition to singing and being at the forefront for the first time, I was also learning to play the keyboard.

Playing the keyboard and singing in front of people was totally out of my element. Learning how to play the keyboard in general was an extreme exercise of faith and not something that I ever thought I would do. Though I was completely out of my comfort zone and stretched like never before; Instead of giving up, I stayed the course, practiced, prayed, and exercised my faith.

Each week I watched as God showed up and blessed our church service. Over time I came to understand that my service as a Christian isn't all about me as God can take the least likely of vessels to use for His glory. Through this process, I also discovered the importance of moving forward regardless of fear, anxiety, and uncertainty.

My defining moment was when I transitioned from struggling to believe that singing was something I could do to fully immersing myself in music. Since that fateful day when I was a young woman gazing out of the kitchen window, I have gone on to write 50 songs, sing on the church praise team, and be a part of several music groups.

My gift for writing eventually led to my writing children's books, movie scripts, and curricula for a nonprofit organization. Even when parts of my journey were difficult and made no sense, I have come to the realization that my trials and struggles were all part of a carefully crafted plan that God had for my life.

In closing, I want to encourage you to find a song in your heart. In other words, that gift, talent, or opportunity that you have been believing God for. Don't be afraid to step out on faith and trust Him. Once you discover your purpose keep moving, praying, believing, and pushing until you reach your goal. You can do all things through Christ who strengthens you!

Pearls of Wisdom

1. When you pray, pray specifically, and don't be afraid to ask God for what you want.

2. God has a plan for your life and will equip you with the tools you need to complete your journey.

3. Once you discover your purpose, keep pushing until you reach your goal.

Nicole L. Crawford

Nicole L. Crawford is a wife, mother of two, and a graduate of Morgan State University. Currently, Nicole resides in Orlando, Florida, and is the Founder and President of a nonprofit organization called C.O.P.E. Mind the Mental Inc.

Nicole is an author and songwriter who has the desire to help others to become the best versions of themselves. In addition to having self-published 3 books, Nicole is the owner and operator of Royalty Kingdom Publishing.

GREAT IS GOD'S FAITHFULNESS

By Pastor Gloria Jolly

L ong before being called into ministry, I had a heart for helping those who were incarcerated, homeless, and struggling with substance abuse, domestic violence, and sexual trauma. Several years ago, I relocated to a new city to accept a position as a Chaplain for a local prison. The opportunity to meet and minister to families and individuals affected by these circumstances was not only my passion but something that God had been preparing me for, for years.

My story starts on a day that was like any other day. I went to work, completed my day, and returned home. There was nothing unusual about this particular day. Later that evening I went to bed, only to be awakened by a sharp, stabbing pain in my abdomen. As the pain intensified, I eventually called 911 and was taken to the hospital.

After a series of tests, I was admitted. The following morning, I was diagnosed with an abdominal blockage that could only be corrected with surgery. It all happened just that quickly. In addition to explaining the upcoming procedures, the doctor informed me that he always prays before his surgeries. I can remember responding, "You are certainly the right man for the job." And he was.

Little did I know that the surgeon's unwavering faith, combined with my own, was about to be put to the ultimate test. Between the multiple surgical procedures that were to come and the long recovery periods in between, the upcoming year would prove to be one of the most challenging years of my life.

In a brief period of just eight months, I would endure more than 97 days in the hospital, comprised of 5 surgical procedures, a stint in the ICU, and a series of unexpected setbacks. Throughout my journey, there were days when it felt as if I was walking through the valley of death. Yet through this experience, my faith would increase in ways I never imagined.

Despite the initial success of the first surgery, the days to follow brought complications that resulted in a month-long stay in the hospital. Upon my discharge, I was home for a few days when I began to experience the same pain. Once again, I was hospitalized and informed that I would need to undergo another surgery due to some additional blockage. Only this time, instead of going home within the days following my surgery I was taken to the Intensive Care Unit.

As a patient in the ICU, I felt helpless and vulnerable and experienced a fear of death that was all too real. This was an unfamiliar space for me considering that throughout my life, I had sung plenty of songs and preached many sermons celebrating the idea of going home to be with God. Despite being fully aware of the scripture verse that says, "to be absent in the body is to be present with the Lord." (2 Corinthians 5:8); In my heart, I knew that I did not want to die.

Coming face to face with my own mortality was nothing short of a sobering experience. There was one day in particular when my faith was really low. I can remember having a conversation with God where I shared my fears about being sick and wondered if I would live to witness another sunrise. It didn't help that I knew of someone who had suffered the same diagnosis that I had just received but did not survive. This example, coupled with the grim faces of the medical staff and the onset of a global pandemic left me with an overwhelming sense of fear that I had never experienced before.

Afraid yet determined to put my trust in God, I cried out to Him expressing my desire to live. Though the months to come would be challenging, the one thing I knew for sure was that my recent move was no coincidence. As my story began to unfold, I knew unequivocally that God had just relocated me to save my life.

I would be less than honest if I didn't mention a few of the harsh realities and uncertainties that go along with battling an illness of this magnitude. The recovery process was long and hard. There were times when I started to feel better, that another setback would come...and another. One setback came in the form of a third surgery that led to my barely being able to do anything for myself unassisted.

By then my body was tired and I hardly had the mental or physical strength to hold on. Thankfully, God is a faithful God who in my moments of fear, pain, and regret held on to me. It was then that I made the conscious decision to trust Him and through this process learned to recognize the hand of God in my life. This was my defining moment.

I won't sugarcoat it... The fight for my healing was intense, requiring consistent effort, and an unwavering determination to survive. Not to mention, it required fervent prayer. From the surgeons down to the hospital janitors, I not only prayed for them regularly but maintained my belief that they were all under the guidance of the Holy Spirit. It is this same faith that helped me to stay positive and remain hopeful, even during my most trying moments.

If you receive nothing else from my story, understand that being a believer or even a minister does not make us exempt from trouble. According to the scripture, "Many are the afflictions of the righteous, but the Lord delivereth him out of them all" (Psalm 34:19). It is during times like this, that it is important to exercise your faith by making your own (personal) declarations to continue to trust God regardless of what your circumstances look like.

At one point, I was reminded of an encounter I had with my grandson. One day, I was sifting through his toys determined to get rid of the ones that I thought were insignificant, broken, outdated, or unnecessary. And without a second thought, I collected these items, tossed them into a garbage bag, and headed to the dumpster to throw them out. That's when my grandson noticed a toy – a blue and gray soldier with missing legs. He took it out of the bag and said he wanted to keep it. Assuming he was joking, I took the toy and tossed it into the dumpster.

It was not until my grandson became visibly upset that I realized how much he cared about the toy. With tears strolling down his face, he uttered the words "I don't care if his legs are missing, I still want him. He means a lot to me."

Here God had used my grandson to impart wisdom that would later comfort me in my hour of need. As I fought to reclaim my life, it wasn't long before I heard the voice of the Lord say, "I will not throw you away." This was a turning point in my recovery.

When everything else around me appeared to be fading, I continued to stand on the promises of God with the full understanding that He would not throw me away. After all this is the same God who had healed me from the sexual abuse and trauma I suffered as a child. The God who gave me the strength to overcome addiction and breast cancer. The God who had sustained me and brought me through surgery, after surgery. God is and has always been faithful.

The more challenging my circumstances became, the more I understood the impact that factors such as faith and persistence had on my healing. Even on days when I didn't feel like participating in therapy, I allowed myself some grace and refused to give up.

Another important part of my healing was choosing not to be persuaded by the negative thoughts and opinions of others. Proverbs 18:21 reminds us, "Death and life are in the power of the tongue, and those who love it will eat its fruit." It's easy to speak about death when there is evidence indicating death as the likely outcome. The real test of our faith is choosing to speak life even in instances alluding to death.

As believers, we have the power and authority to speak life or death into existence. Words are powerful. Understanding this power and choosing to "walk by faith" and "not by sight" during difficult times helps us to manifest the tomorrow we desire based on the words we speak over ourselves today.

For the lonely times that were ahead, I took a proactive approach toward establishing a support system of people that I could reach out to when I needed encouragement. Even with the occasional visit from in-home nurses, I would often find myself alone and isolated for extended periods. Though I was still not well enough to drive, I came to appreciate the convenience of being able to communicate with others via phone and email.

Before I knew it, I was reaching out regularly to check on other people. I noticed that when I shifted the focus from my own problems to praying and helping others, some of the very things I worried about seemed to pale in comparison to the trials and tribulations of other people.

By praying for someone else, checking in on them, or sending a meal to a homebound individual, I was reminded of how fortunate I was to be alive. Slowly but surely my health was improving, and putting the needs of others ahead of my own gave me a fresh perspective and the strength to carry on.□

Over time, even the medical professionals who were once fearful that I would not survive my ordeal would later be inspired by my faith and determination to live. Reflecting on my life, I am grateful that God has been there since the beginning. He knew that the hardships I would go on to face would not break me, but rather shape me into the person I am today. God knows everything about us and loves us unconditionally, despite our imperfections and mistakes. Through Jesus, God has provided a solution for all of our sins, past, present, and future. It is because of Jesus that I am healed.

When I look back and reflect on this period of my life, I am reminded of the time I was going through labor to deliver my son. Similar to my growth in ministry, the labor pains increased as the delivery drew near. Simple tasks became harder, such as tying my shoes, sleeping through the night, and maintaining my energy.

Similarly, in the spiritual realm, obstacles multiply when we become a threat to the enemy. The moment I committed to live a life of honor to God, I started encountering new challenges that were previously unfamiliar to me. Instead of viewing them as traps, I learned to perceive these hurdles as opportunities to increase my faith in God.

As stated in God's word "Teach me to do thy will; for thou art my God: thy spirit is good; lead me into the land of uprightness." (Psalm 143:10). Every obstacle that comes my way now serves as a sign that I am on the right path.

With God, all things are possible. Even when we try to accomplish things on our own strength and fail, God remains faithful. While some challenges may seem insurmountable, we must remember that Jesus declared, "Let's go to the other side..." (Luke 8:22) regardless of the storm that was coming. His focus was always on the destination, not the distractions along the way. We too must remain confident in His promise that if He said we will reach our destination, we will.

This experience has taught me some valuable lessons and strengthened my faith. Though the journey to healing and wholeness can be difficult, it can also be rewarding. To summarize my thoughts and emotions surrounding God, I am grateful for His faithfulness throughout this journey. As I reflect on the many times when God has proven to be faithful still, I will forever remember this season. The season when I was challenged, stretched, proven, and tried. Great is God's faithfulness.

Pearls of Wisdom:

1. God knows exactly what is needed in each of our lives to draw us closer to Him and His will.

2. God is faithful and will finish the good work that he has started in you. The process isn't always easy, but it is worthwhile.

3. Every aspect of our lives is permitted or performed by God. Therefore, we can trust Him and find comfort in knowing that He is still in control.

Pastor Gloria Jolly

Pastor Gloria Jolly is a Certified Recovery Peer Specialist, with specialization in Human Resources. She is also a Certified Addiction and Awareness educator and has served as Chaplain for the Wakulla Correctional Institution in North Florida. As Chief Servant of Keepers of the Flock Ministry, her ministry provides outreach to the homeless, domestic violence survivors, substance abusers, individuals and families impacted by HIV/AIDS, as well as those who are incarcerated. Additionally, she is the founder of Hope for Today Ministry, which equips the body of Christ with addiction awareness, education, effective prayer, and life coaching.

An ordained pastor and prophetess, with a bachelor's degree in theology, as well as associate degrees in biblical and general studies. Pastor Jolly completed her training at Soaring Eagles School of the Prophets. Currently, she serves as an ordained minister at Christ Dominion Church Fellowship. Her list of affiliations includes Greater Kingdom Alliance Fellowship, NAMI, and ICARE.

Pastor Jolly's ministry has taken her all over the United States and beyond. In addition, she is passionate about helping homeless veterans and hopes to open a center to provide housing, services, reconciliation, and hope to those who have faithfully served our country but are now displaced.

Pastor Jolly is the mother of David Jolly and grandmother of Jonathan Jolly. Through her faith and dedication, she continues to make a difference in the lives of those who need it.

NO OBSTACLE TOO BIG

By Taylor Daniels

I was 16 years old when the positive pregnancy test I held in my hand shattered the denial I used as a shield to protect me from giving in to fear and anxiety. My father had such high hopes for my sister and I as his only children. The very thought of disappointing him had been among my greatest fears for some time. Running through my mind were questions about my future. Even worse, what were my parents going to think?

Though the father of my child was a good person, at the time there were no guarantees that he would be around for the long run. Raised by a single mother I knew better than to fantasize about living life happily ever after. Instead, I had been taught at a young age to be self-sufficient and understood that it was going to take a lot of hard work and determination to secure a future for myself and my child.

The more I thought about the road ahead, the more distraught I became. My future, my dreams, and the things I had often daydreamed about didn't seem to matter anymore. I lost hope and spent many nights engulfed in negative thoughts and among them was fears about my pregnancy.

Though it was long before I became pregnant, it's difficult to pinpoint when the bouts of sadness first began. The fact that I had been bullied and ostracized at school had been a major factor impacting my mental and emotional well-being. Not knowing what to do, I suffered in silence and was in the 6th grade when I wrote my first goodbye letter and started imagining how much better things would be if I wasn't around anymore. I functioned this way for many years as no one seemed to notice.

I had an overwhelming sense of fear and anxiety that would often prevent me from being comfortable around others to the degree that I didn't participate in school sports or activities. By age 16, and even before expecting, I had already contemplated suicide. I wasn't safe or happy where I lived and was confused about some of the things that were happening to me. Things that I now understand to be sexual assault. Once again, I suffered in silence. Not having a stable support system at the time seemed to amplify the negative emotions I was experiencing. Emotions that I would later come to identify as depression.

Depression does not care who you are, how much or how little you have, or even how old you are. It comes and hits you sometimes without you even knowing you are suffering from it. It's dark, empty, and lonely. Depression can make you believe that you don't need people in your life and will cause you to end up shutting some important people out. It makes you think that you can't physically move, or emotionally feel anything. It attacks from every angle and will leave you in despair. It's a deep, painful, and gut-wrenching feeling and something that I have struggled with for most of my life.

Learning that I was pregnant left me with feelings of hopelessness on top of already feeling alone, unloved, and unprotected. It was truly a low point in my life and a time when I seriously contemplated ending it all to the extent of envisioning how, when, and where it would happen as well as how I wanted my funeral services to go.

With the help of my sister and child's father, I was able to finish high school while pregnant. My stepmother taught me to drive and helped me to get my license, and my mother allowed me to use her car to get back and forth to alternative school which turned out to be a lot better for me. Though I was still living with my mother, I managed to find work earning a minimum wage, but it was income, nonetheless.

Later that year, I gave birth to a beautiful baby boy. I can't describe the fear I felt in knowing that I was going to be a young mother. However, when I first held my son, I experienced something that I had never felt before that I can only describe as a moment of clarity. I knew instantly that this child had just saved my life.

Giving birth to my son was the defining moment in my life in which I knew that I needed to get myself together. It wasn't just me anymore. Someone was depending on me now. To this day I can remember the first time I breastfeed my son when the thought suddenly occurred to me "I am literally this child's life source right now". This little, tiny, human is depending on me. I am his mother! When my son looked up at me, I found fulfillment in knowing that I may not be a perfect person in the eyes of the world, but in the eyes of my son, I was everything. For the first time in my life, I realized that I was enough.

Leaving the hospital with my son restored my faith and hope for the future. The first order of business was to decide what I was going to do to take care of us. I knew I wanted a career and was determined more than ever to be somebody for us. I decided to follow my dream of becoming a social worker or counselor for teenage girls like me. A career in which I could be the person I needed when I was growing up.

When I returned to school, I took my classes seriously and was able to graduate from high school a few months earlier than my class. An accomplishment that I was extremely proud of. Due to some unpaid fees, I was deemed ineligible to participate in the graduation ceremony but lived close enough to the school to hear the cheers of my classmates graduating. Not being able to walk across the stage was devasting. At that moment I made a promise to myself that I would one day finish college and experience the pride of walking across the stage as a college graduate.

Shortly after finishing high school, I enrolled in college and started on my journey toward earning a degree in Criminal Justice. It was another proud moment even though attending college was no easy task. The school was over an hour away and the daily train ride was about $12 round trip. There were people from all walks of life, experiences that challenged me, and days when depression and anxiety kicked in. Yet I was determined to finish what I started.

I was two years into the program when the college I was attending lost its accreditation and closed due to fraud. There I was with a mountain of student debt, a bookcase full of college textbooks, papers stained with tears and sweat, and no degree to show for it. Now I would have to start all over again. I hadn't felt that defeated in a long time. Unfortunately, I was defeated to the point of giving up.

Though it wasn't fulfilling, I found work at a call center. Several months later my son's father and I were married. After suffering a miscarriage, I eventually gave birth to another son. Life was hard and we struggled as a family for a long time. I can remember having days when I thought to myself "This can't be it." "This" as in the cycle of taking out loans, borrowing money, having our vehicles repossessed, moving in and out of our relatives' homes, and always needing help.

I have often heard it said that insanity is "doing the same thing over and over again while expecting different results." Whatever "this" was, it was starting to take its toll on our family. My husband and I both knew that we were living lives that were less than what we deserved. Most of all, we both knew that something needed to change. Tired of repeating the same cycle, my husband made the difficult decision to leave for trucking school.

At that point in our marriage, I had just given birth to a baby girl. My husband would be gone for months. This would be the first time we were ever apart. How was I supposed to manage everything alone while he was gone? Initially, it was a plan that seemed impossible. As I would soon learn, however, "With God all things are possible" (Matthew 19:26).

I was 25 years old and a mother of three when I decided it was time to go back to college to pursue the dreams I once had. I pushed past the notion that I was too old, after realizing that I would be 30 years old by the time I finished. I wasn't getting any younger and knew if I didn't go back to school then, at some point in the future I would live to regret it.

This time, I had a strong support system including an aunt who has since become my best friend and mentor. It was through this connection that I realized that there is absolutely nothing I can't do. Regardless of having started my journey as a teenage mother, I finally realized that my life wasn't over. It was still possible for my family to live in a home that we own, and for us to go on vacations like regular people. Even in my struggles, I came to realize that it was still possible for me to have the life I've always dreamed of. Only, I would no longer dream. From that moment on I aspired.

I enrolled in college, once again pursuing my bachelor's degree in criminal justice. To maintain my focus, I set time limits for my goals and started to achieve them slowly but surely. Being that my husband was still on the road and only home a few days out of the month; this left me alone to manage two kids, a newborn, a full-time job, and a dog coupled with being a full-time student. I would be less than honest if I didn't admit to being tired every day. However, the drive and determination within me were stronger than any thoughts I had of quitting.

During this new phase of my life when I realized that I could conquer just about anything, I decided it was also time to reclaim my mental peace as well. This included improving the relationship I had with my mother which had been strained since my childhood. I also decided to improve my relationship with God, and through this journey developed a self-awareness that helped me to heal from things that I could never talk about.

Perhaps the most important lesson I learned came from my Aunt which is the power of the word "no". For years I watched in awe as she stood up for herself. It was then that I began my journey of self-love and respect, which should have started a long time ago. From that moment on I said "no" to split birthday parties for my kids to accommodate divorced parents. I said "no" to splitting holidays, and "no" to putting my feelings and myself on the back burner to alleviate other people's feelings. It was past time that I started thinking about my peace and what that meant for me.

My college years became years of self-exploring and learning that I could achieve what I used to think was impossible. During this time, I sought therapy and went to the doctor to improve my health. Still experiencing severe bouts of depression, I was finally diagnosed with Premenstrual Dysphoric Disorder (PMDD) which is a hormonal condition that occurs frequently around my monthly cycle. Having a better understanding of the issue that had plagued me since childhood also gave me hope that it was something that I could overcome. With a little prayer and patience, thankfully I did.

It wasn't long before things started looking up for our family. My husband was home, and we were finally able to purchase our first house. It was hard work, but well worth it when we pulled into the driveway of the home that I never allowed myself to believe that we could have. Apartment life had long trained us to be quiet because of the neighbors, and I will never forget the feeling of telling our children that it was okay for them to run, jump, scream, and make as much noise as they wanted. It felt amazing to finally have something of our own.

Two years later I graduated from college with a bachelor's degree in criminal justice. Earning my degree meant everything to me. Due to the pandemic, I was not able to walk across a stage. However, my family rented out a movie theater to watch the virtual ceremony on the big screen and I was able to walk across the theater floor when my name was called. It was an emotional moment that represented every single hope and dream I had held onto since I was 16 years old. For me, this degree was a symbol of the future that I finally secured for my children. Seeing how proud they were of me as their mother was a full-circle moment.

Through all the pain, downfalls, and disappointments, God made a way by ensuring that no obstacle was too big for me to walk into the fullness of the plans and purposes he had for me. By the grace of God, I knew if I kept going nothing would stand in my way. After graduation, I started working as a guard in a juvenile facility. Within six months, I stepped out on faith and applied for a position in the probation department and got the job! After operating in my new role for a year, I knew without a doubt that I was exactly where I was supposed to be.

Today I am pursuing the career of my dreams while completing a master's degree in criminal justice. I have come a long way from the 16-year-old girl who didn't fully know how or if she would make it; to becoming a woman that I can truly be proud of. Even in that, I want to be clear that this is not a success story as I am still a work in progress.

The one thing this journey has taught me is that there is no obstacle too big for God. Whatever situation you may be in, know that God has a plan even in those times when you can't see it in all the darkness. Life can be hard sometimes, and if you ever find yourself in a situation where you feel you are not enough, focus on the people who love and care about you. If for nothing else, push through for them. You'll be glad you did. I know I am.

Pearls of Wisdom:

1. If something does not feel right with your health or mental state, never be ashamed to seek medical attention.

2. A person being your family member is not a green light for them to hurt you. Establish boundaries for the sake of your peace and happiness. It doesn't matter if the person is a sibling, grandparent, or even a parent; blood is not an excuse for painful actions, and you do not have to tolerate it.

3. Always celebrate your accomplishments, even if they are small ones. It's easy to be hard on yourself. Learn to be positive and speak words of affirmation over your life.

Taylor Daniels

Taylor Daniels is a mother of three beautiful children. Born and raised in Waukegan, Illinois, she now lives in Corpus Christi, Texas. Her passion for criminal justice and helping troubled youth has led to a successful career as a juvenile probation officer for Nueces County.

Additionally, Taylor has earned a bachelor's degree in criminal justice with a concentration in Legal Studies and Advocacy from Southern New Hampshire University in 2021. Currently, she is pursuing her master's degree and remains optimistic and driven to make a difference in the lives of the youth she serves.

BIRTHING A CAN'T

By Kimberly N. Johnson

When the average 23-year-old thinks about the future, most envision nothing but life ahead of them, naturally assuming that there will be plenty of time to live, change, and make dreams come true. At that age, I was no exception. I was young, single, working, and living on my own without a care in the world when suddenly life as I knew it came to a screeching halt.

I hadn't been feeling well for some time. Breathing had become difficult, and everyday activities such as showering and putting on shoes would often leave me feeling exhausted. Even the simple act of resting flat on my back in bed was no longer possible for me. One night, I woke unexpectedly, drenched in sweat, and feeling like an elephant was sitting on my chest. It was extremely scary and resulted in a trip to the emergency room.

Confused and terrified, I would soon learn that had I not sought medical attention that night, it is likely that I would have suffocated in my sleep. After a barrage of tests and questions, finally an explanation in three life-altering words... Congestive Heart Failure. Being admitted into the hospital with the understanding that the condition of my heart was comparable to that of a person nearly four times my age was a lot to take in. At the time I didn't know much only that my life was about to change.

The pity party I hosted for myself was epic and started with a pre-celebration of worry over the possibility of surgery, followed by a jam session of anguish in tribute to the daily medications that I would be taking to reduce the excess fluid in my body. Let's not forget the celebration of frustration over the low-sodium diet that would become a crucial part of sustaining my life; and for the grand finale... cue in the sadness in honor of the realization that at just 23 years old, I needed a cardiologist.

Of course, no party would be complete without music. In the background, the gloomy lyrics of my pain and anxiety played on repeat like a broken record... "Why me? I'm too young. It isn't fair." "Why me? I'm too young. It isn't fair." "Why me? I'm too young. It isn't fair..."

If being informed that I would be on heart medications for the remainder of my life was not enough, my life expectancy at the time was estimated by doctors to be five years or maybe ten if I stuck to the program. Most devastating, I was told that I would not be able to have children due to the risks (some of which are fatal) associated with my condition.

My faith in the Lord had always been strong and would not allow me to waiver or dwell on the news that I had just been given. Instead, I prayed, and the Holy Spirit answered with a promise that I would indeed experience motherhood with at least one child. Shortly after, I was discharged from the hospital; leaving with a level of peace and gratitude that I had never experienced before.

If I was going to survive, I knew that I had work to do. Starting with my mindset, as there was no time for pity parties or negative thoughts. I was in the fight of my life and understood almost immediately that the changes I needed to make were not going to be easy. In addition to a low-sodium diet, my treatment consisted of exercise and a daily routine of medications with the understanding that a cure was not a possibility.

Several years later, I was thriving and had just started seeing a new cardiologist when I learned that having a child was indeed possible. By then I was married to a man who had a child from a previous relationship and up to that point I had often wondered if being a stepmom would be my only path to motherhood.

After exploring the possibilities of a successful pregnancy, my husband and I started trying to conceive immediately. Despite having invested in tools to include ovulation test strips and a mobile app, three years had come and gone, and still no baby. Each month had become one disappointment after the next, yet I held on to the promise that had been made by God in my hospital room all those years ago.

One summer day that started like any other, I knew something was different. I had been feeling ill all week and decided to take a pregnancy test. I could hardly contain my emotions when I discovered that the test was positive. I began rejoicing and praising God, not to mention thinking of a creative way to share the news with my husband who was ecstatic and over the moon once he found out.

The early part of my pregnancy was shrouded in fear and uncertainty which slowly diminished the further the pregnancy progressed. I can remember the first time I saw my baby on the ultrasound. The doctor laughed at the sight of the baby leaping on the screen just as Elizabeth's baby had leaped in her womb (Luke 1:41). For me, experiencing that moment further confirmed that our baby was special and meant to be.

My Cardiologist had warned us in advance that my pregnancy would have to be closely monitored and it was. The pregnancy was considered high risk and it didn't help that my heart showed signs of weakness, coupled with my having developed gestational diabetes. Though the weekly appointments rotating between the obstetrician and cardiologist had become exhausting, I was beyond grateful for the experience. Overall, the baby and I were doing great, even though our prognosis on paper appeared grim.

It wasn't long before we learned that we were having a baby girl. As fate would have it, we had found out we were pregnant on my grandmother's birthday and had learned the sex of the baby on my grandfather's birthday. We decided early on that the baby's first name and initials would honor her paternal grandfather and great-great-great-great-grandmother on the maternal side; and that the meaning of her middle name would be "God's promise" in honor of God and all He has done.

On the day our daughter was due to arrive, I was nervous but never stopped praying or believing God for my blessing. I was scheduled for induced labor, however, my contractions started early, and before I knew it, my water broke. Although I had planned to give birth naturally, complications arose, and I ended up having a C-section.

When my baby girl was finally placed on my shoulder, I noticed that she wasn't crying.

Soon after the birth, we were separated. My daughter was taken to the NICU, and I was moved to a room where I was reunited with my immediate family. Beyond being told that the baby had gone without oxygen and was lethargic, I wasn't given much information aside from a phone number with a code that I could call to check in on her.

Due to the condition of my health and the health of the baby, I was not permitted to see my daughter for four long days. Meanwhile, I immediately resumed taking heart medications that had been deemed too harmful to take during the pregnancy which also meant that I would not be able to breastfeed my baby.

In a separate part of the hospital, my daughter was receiving cooling therapy (Neonatal Therapeutic Hypothermia) to minimize the risk of brain damage. It was a terrifying feeling but a reminder to continue to pray for my child just as I had from the moment, I first saw the two lines appear on the pregnancy test.

While we were apart, my husband was able to visit our daughter and would bring back pictures and videos of her progress all of which were extremely comforting. After countless prayers and a few sleepless nights, I soon learned that the cooling therapy had been successful and that I would finally be able to see my daughter.

For me, no embrace has ever been as sweet as the one I experienced the day I held her. As mother and daughter, we were finally together and for the first time in our ordeal, could truly rest. It would be a few days before we would be able to go home. Even then I knew that there was a strong possibility that we had a long road ahead of us.

Following our discharge from the hospital we visited several specialists to rule out Cerebral Palsy. One specialist after another my daughter was given a clean bill of health. The fact that my daughter was even here was a far cry from the "can't" doctors had spoken a decade before. Once again, God had shown Himself strong.

Becoming a mother and "birthing a can't" was the defining moment of my life. Even when the odds were stacked against me, I held on to my faith, and by the grace of God, I received a miracle in the form of a beautiful daughter who was born a fighter and survivor. Together we have faced many challenges. Yet, I refused to be shaken and have chosen the path of courage with every issue we faced.

Hebrews 11:6 tells us "But without faith it is impossible to please Him, for he who comes to God must believe that He is, and that He is a rewarder of those who diligently seek Him." In sharing my story, I hope to inspire those who are faced with insurmountable struggles to find peace and refuge in the almighty arms of our heavenly father.

It is in times of adversity that we should remember that God is stronger than any problem or obstacle we may face. This is why it is important to be prayerful when situations arise, particularly in the form of a "can't". Some of life's greatest trials and sufferings are steppingstones to greatness.

Pearls of Wisdom:

1. We must be prayerful when situations are presented to us and remember that God's plans and purposes for us extend beyond earthly conclusions.

2. Some of God's greatest miracles start with a "can't". Therefore, never allow anything or anyone to convince you that something isn't possible.

3. Turn a pity party into a worship experience honoring God and thanking him for all that He has done, is doing, and will do in your life, and never forget that God has the final say.

Kimberly N. Johnson

Kimberly N. Johnson is a mother, Christian, and life coach who currently resides in Birmingham, Alabama with her daughter Mariah, and loving mother, Barbara. Blessed with the gift of exhortation, Kimberly is the founder of several ministry initiatives including Unveiled Silhouette, When Helpmates Need Help, and COB (Close Of Business) with Coach KimmieJ.

Kimberly would like to dedicate this chapter to her grandmother Eunice Delois, who challenged her to not just exist but live. Live your life to the fullest and create beautiful memories. That's what Eunice Delois believed, and that's how she lived.

The name Eunice means "good victory". Victory is an act of defeating an enemy in battle. In Kimberly's own words, " I declare victory for each person who comes across this inspiring anthology."

THROUGH MY EYES

By Angela Salter

As far back as my earliest memories, God was always a part of my life. As a child, I attended church services regularly where I developed an awareness of God, though it would be much later in life that I would fully come to understand the magnitude of His power. This story is a glimpse of God's mercy and grace that I experienced during some of the most difficult times in my life. My journey of hope and salvation... Through my eyes.

My childhood wasn't always easy. My home life had been dark and lonely, and I always dreaded seeing the streetlights come on which for a child of my generation usually meant that it was time to journey home. Having a full understanding of the turmoil that often awaited me, there were times when I would steal, act out, and even run away to avoid the misery of returning to that place.

By the tender age of thirteen, sexual abuse and trauma whether it was at the hands of a family member or friend of the family, had become commonplace and with no end in sight. Naïve I would often blame myself wondering if factors such as my appearance or parts of my behavior contributed to my being targeted and violated by different men as often as the abuse occurred.

In addition to the shame associated with sexual abuse, it had become increasingly difficult to endure the punishments that were severe and had long become routine. Often afraid, I had no friends or anyone I could trust or turn to. I hated the things that were happening to me and felt confused as to why as a child I had to suffer in this way. It was then that I started crying out to God even while questioning if He was even real.

Though I didn't realize it at the time, God's protection and answer to my prayers came in the form of an unexpected move to live with a relative in a different state. Moving to a different state was a fresh start and a chance to heal from the wounds of the past. Yet at the age of 14, I was still very broken and prone to acting out.

Relocating to a new state didn't make me less of a target for child predators, however, it was the first sense of normalcy I had ever experienced in all my life. Like a typical teenager, I still made mistakes and for a long time held on to anger, and even now as an adult I still sometimes grieve for the little girl in me who didn't have anyone to protect her.

In my new life, God was still a part of my journey. By then, I knew without a doubt that it was God who had kept me, and He who still loved me no matter how far I strayed from Him. As a teen, I attended church services regularly furthering my relationship with Christ, a foundation of which I would need for all that was to come.

The effects of my childhood trauma would stay with me for years and would shape the way that I view myself and men. I would go on to graduate from high school, but not before becoming pregnant during my senior year of high school. At the age of 18, I gave birth to a beautiful baby boy who attended my graduation the following spring. As much as I wanted to make it work with my child's father, our relationship did have its share of problems.

From the time I had my son, I knew almost immediately that being a mother was going to be hard. What I didn't know was how hard living with his father (who struggled with addiction) would be. Living with a drug addict was both frightening and chaotic. There were days when the lights and water were off and essentials such as money and food were in short supply. After our second son was born, I made the difficult decision to leave with the children.

As I would soon learn, being a single mother was even harder. However, nothing could prepare me for the pain I experienced the day that I lost my youngest son who died suddenly from SIDS (Sudden Infant Death Syndrome). Losing a child is a painful experience that I will never forget. It's a pain that leaves you feeling crippled and leaves your mind reeling in a perpetual cycle of grief and shock.

Losing a child was a real test of my faith and left me wondering why so many horrible things had happened to me. When would this horrible cycle be broken? Why did God allow this to happen? Had I strayed too far from the Father? Even now I'm still now sure how I made it through, I only know that there were days when I would have lost my mind had it not been for the grace of God.

After the death of our son, his father and I reunited briefly to cope with the loss. Even then, there was still the matter of his addiction. Between money going missing, utilities being shut off, and not being able to trust him with our child; our union was short-lived but not before learning that I was pregnant yet again with our third child, a son.

Over time, I began to live again and knew without a shadow of a doubt that God had kept me. By the time I was in my forties, I had survived one failed marriage and several toxic relationships, one of which I had suffered abuse and domestic violence; another that blessed me with a beautiful daughter. Fully embracing life as a single mother, I maintained a home, along with a successful career, and was heavily involved in the church. For the first time, life was goo d.

Years later, tragedy would strike once again when my oldest son was shot in the head. Though the bullet struck and shattered an eye, by the grace of God, he lived. My son lived. Even amid my grief and anxiety over what happened to my son, I praised God for sparing me from the pain and anguish of not having to bury another child. God had been merciful and true to His word. For this, I give Him praise.

Through it all, (sexual abuse, domestic violence, and the loss of a child...) I have discovered a love unlike anything I have ever experienced before. Which is the love of God. Deuteronomy 31:8, tells us that "It is the Lord that goes before you. He will be with you; He will not leave you or forsake you. Do not fear or be dismayed." I was well into my adulthood when I finally came to understand what it truly means to be a child of God.

Life for me hasn't always been easy. Yet, through it all, I held on to my faith and never stopped believing that God would see me through. In Christ, I'm delivered and free from the guilt and shame of my past. I am no longer bound to the poor choices and negative thoughts that once plagued me and held me in bondage. For these reasons and more, I will continue to serve Him.

Today I stand tall, no longer ashamed, and proud of the person I have become. In Christ, I have learned to love myself and see myself through His eyes. No matter how far I drifted away, God has never ceased to welcome me and continues to cover me with his mercy and grace to this very day. The same mercy and grace will cover you also.

If you are suffering from tragedy, devastation, or mistakes from the past... Don't lose hope, but instead trust God. Tomorrow is a new day. Brighter days are ahead and by His Grace, you will begin to see yourself through God's eyes.

Pearls of Wisdom:

1. Seek God for strength, courage, hope, and self-love to see yourself through His eyes.

2. You are not bound by the sins of the past. God has the power to restore and heal you from your brokenness.

3. No matter how far you have fallen, God will never leave you and will always welcome you with open arms.

Angela Salter

Angela Salter is a mother, grandmother, and resident of Tampa, Florida. With over 35 years of experience in the service industry and 25 years of volunteer work in her community, Angela Salter is an exceptional individual. Her unwavering faith, which began at the age of 14, has helped her navigate through the ups and downs of life.

Despite facing challenges and obstacles, Angela believes that going through difficult times is necessary to reach the promises of God. Most of all, she is confident that with His guidance, she can overcome anything and proudly proclaim, "God did it!"

Angela Salter is the founder of Pursuing Purpose Ministries dedicated to spreading the Gospel of Jesus Christ and inspiring people to find their purpose.

AFTERWORD

This book was a labor of love showcasing the incredible stories of women who have faced adversity and come out stronger on the other side. These women opened their hearts, sharing their trials and tribulations, their fears and doubts, and ultimately their triumphs, hoping readers will be inspired by their bravery and resilience.

From the first-time author to the seasoned writer, they all share a common thread of courage and determination that is truly inspiring. Their stories cover a wide range of topics, from overcoming illness, abuse, and trauma to navigating difficult circumstances and pursuing their dreams. Through their words, these women offer a message of hope to anyone who may be struggling with their own challenges. They show us that even in difficult moments, there is always a way forward and that we are capable of achieving great things if we are willing to persevere and trust God even in times of darkness and struggle.

Dr. Aleta V. Ashford